The Path to Business Ownership

A Comprehensive Guide to Franchising and Solopreneurship Inspiration, Guidance, and Actionable Tools to Bring Your Vision to Life

Kenneth M. Rollins

All rights reserved. No part of this publication may be reproduced, distributed, or transmitted in any form or by any means, including photocopying, recording, or other electronic or mechanical methods, without the prior written permission of the publisher, except in the case of brief quotations embodied in critical reviews and certain other noncommercial uses permitted by copyright law.
Copyright © (Kenneth M. Rollins), (2024).

Table of Contents

Introduction 1

Chapter 1: Dreaming Big: Unlocking the Entrepreneurial Spirit 6

Chapter 2: Choosing Your Path: Franchising vs. Solopreneurship 14

Chapter 3: Market Research and Finding Your Niche 23

Chapter 4: Developing a Winning Business Plan 33

Chapter 5: Navigating Franchising: What to Look For 42

Chapter 6: The Solopreneur Mindset: Building from the Ground Up 51

Chapter 7: Essential Tools and Resources for Entrepreneurs 59

Chapter 8: Legal, Financial, and Administrative Essentials 70

Chapter 9: Building a Team and Scaling Your Business 80

Chapter 10: Staying Inspired: Long-Term Success and Fulfillment 90

Conclusion 100

Appendix 106

Introduction

One of the most compelling goals for many individuals is to start their own company. It signifies individuality, creativity, and the chance to create something significant. Whether it's the appeal of financial independence, the opportunity to follow a passion, or the desire to leave a legacy, the entrepreneurial route is one of the most rewarding—and challenging—journeys a person can take.

However, taking the initial step might be intimidating. Should you invest in a tried-and-true system by becoming a franchisee, or should you start your own business as a solopreneur? Both pathways have distinct possibilities and difficulties, and the best decision is based on your objectives, talents, and future vision. This book will help you explore those alternatives and offer you the inspiration, encouragement, and practical skills you need to make your goal a reality.

Why this guide?

Starting a company entails more than simply taking a risk; it also requires planning, strategy, and execution. This book is your partner on that journey, providing concrete guidance and insights suited to ambitious entrepreneurs exploring franchising or solopreneurship. Unlike many business manuals, which concentrate primarily on one model, this handbook compares both possibilities, allowing you to make an educated selection.

This guide will assist you:

Understand the advantages and disadvantages of franchising over solopreneurship.

Develop the mentality and abilities required for business success.

Navigate the complexity of market research, financial planning, and legal compliance.

Prepare yourself with skills and tactics for overcoming obstacles and thriving.

Who is this guide for?

This article is for everyone who has ever wanted to be their boss but isn't sure how to start. Whether you're leaving a corporate job, pursuing financial independence, or just searching for a means to convert your passion into profit, this book is for you.

Aspiring Franchise Owners: If you want to work inside a proven system with existing branding and operational assistance, this book will help you assess franchise prospects, comprehend agreements, and thrive in a structured business environment.

Future Solopreneurs: If you want the freedom to start your own company, this book will help you create a brand, expand your offerings, and deal with the problems of being a one-person powerhouse.

What You Will Learn

Throughout this book, we'll cover crucial issues that any prospective business owner should know:

How do you make your company objectives consistent with your own beliefs and lifestyle?

Strategies for selecting the best franchise or developing a distinctive solopreneurs enterprise.

Required abilities for market research, financial planning, and company operations.

Tips for tackling typical challenges, ranging from

obtaining capital to expanding your firm.

But this advice goes beyond the practical. It also tackles the emotional and psychological sides of business, such as building confidence, staying motivated, and navigating the inevitable ups and downs.

The promise of entrepreneurship

Becoming a company owner is more than simply generating money. It is about leading a life of purpose and fulfillment. It's about taking charge of your future, realizing your full potential, and creating something that represents your vision.

The journey to company ownership is not always simple, but it is always worthwhile. With the correct preparation, mentality, and support, you can overcome challenges, grasp chances, and realize your ambitions.

This guide will assist you every step of the way.

So let us get started. Whether you're interested in the organized prospects of franchising or the creative flexibility of solopreneurship, your path starts now.

Chapter 1: Dreaming Big: Unlocking the Entrepreneurial Spirit

Every successful company begins with a dream—a vision of something more than what is presently available. Dreaming big is the cornerstone of entrepreneurship, the fuel that motivates people to live lives of purpose, passion, and freedom. However, dreaming alone is not sufficient. To turn your dreams into a successful company, you must first unleash your entrepreneurial spirit, understand what motivates you, and overcome the anxieties that often keep you back.

Understanding Your Motivations for Business Ownership.

Entrepreneurship is as varied as the individuals who choose to pursue it. Some are driven by financial independence, eager to break free from the confines of a 9-to-5 employment. Others are motivated by a desire to create, whether via a product, service, or legacy. Understanding your motives is the first step towards creating a company that reflects your beliefs and long-term objectives.

Questions To Ask Yourself:

Why do you want to start a business? Is it to get out of a bad circumstance, to realize a long-held desire, or to prosper financially?

What does success look like for me? Is it about accumulating riches, making a difference, or living a balanced life?

What am I prepared to give up to make this happen? Entrepreneurship often involves time, effort, and financial commitment.

By delving thoroughly into these questions, you might begin to find the fundamental "why" of your business goals. This clarity is critical since your motives will help you navigate the obstacles and uncertainties of company ownership.

Identifying and aligning your passions with potential ventures

Passion is the flame that sparks creativity and drives persistence. The most successful entrepreneurs often begin with something they really care about—an issue they want to solve, a pastime they want to monetize, or a cause they want to promote. However, enthusiasm alone does not ensure success. It must be consistent with a realistic market opportunity.

Steps for Discovering and Aligning Your Passions:

1. Identify Your Interests and Skills:

Which activities provide you joy?

What skills or abilities do you have that others value?

What kind of issues do you normally lean towards solving?

2. Research Market Demand:

Are there any holes in the market that correspond to your interests?

Who are your prospective clients and what are their needs?

How does your concept provide value or address a problem?

3. Align Passion with Practicality:

Determine the viability of your ideas in terms of resources, time, and effort.

Consider sectors in which your interests coincide with trends and opportunities.

Consider scalability—can your firm expand over time?

By combining your passion with a clear business opportunity, you may build an enterprise that is both rewarding and financially viable.

Overcome Common Fears and Doubts

For many ambitious entrepreneurs, fear is the most significant barrier to launching a firm. Fear of failure, fear of the unknown, and even fear of achievement may paralyze you before you ever get started. The key to conquering these concerns is to approach them directly and reframe them as possibilities for progress.

Common Fears and Ways to Address Them:

1. Fear of failure:

Reframe It: Failure is not the end; it is a learning opportunity. Many successful businesses failed many times before becoming successful.

Take little steps. Break down your trip into doable stages. Celebrate your progress, no matter how tiny.

2. Fear of Financial Risks:

Plan thoroughly: Prepare a precise financial strategy and budget. Identify measures to reduce risk, such as beginning small or looking for alternate financing sources.

Seek Support: Surround yourself with mentors, advisers, or a support network to help you.

3. Fear of the unknown:

Educate Yourself: Learn everything you can about your industry, competition, and market. Knowledge minimizes uncertainty.

Embrace Uncertainty: Accept that not every aspect will be flawless. Entrepreneurs value flexibility.

4. Fear of success:

Recognize It: Success often comes with more accountability and visibility. Recognize the changes and prepare for them.

Stay grounded by focussing on your objective and the positive effect of your company.

Increasing Confidence and Resilience:

Visualise Success: Imagine yourself attaining your objectives. Visualization promotes a good outlook.

Practice Self-Compassion: Entrepreneurship is a journey rather than a destination. Be nice to yourself, and learn from your errors.

Seek Inspiration: Research other entrepreneurs who overcome similar concerns. Their tales may inspire and comfort you.

Dreaming Big, Acting Bold.
Dreaming big is the first step, but action is what makes dreams a reality. Unlocking your entrepreneurial spirit entails taking purposeful measures to understand your motivations, matching your interests with possibilities, and confronting your anxieties with bravery and commitment.

Your entrepreneurship experience is unique to you. It's a difficult route, but one that has enormous possibilities. By thinking big and planning meticulously, you may position yourself to build a company that not only accomplishes your objectives but also inspires others along the way.

So, take a deep breath, believe in your goal, and move ahead. The world is waiting for your ideas, enthusiasm, and distinctive contributions. It's your turn to shine.

Chapter 2: Choosing Your Path: Franchising vs. Solopreneurship

The choice to start a company is life-changing, but the route you pursue will influence the rest of your journey. Do you invest in a franchise's structure and assistance, or do you go solo and establish your own business? Both pathways offer advantages and disadvantages, and recognizing the fundamental distinctions will help you choose the choice that best suits your ambitions, lifestyle, and objectives.

This chapter will go over the advantages and disadvantages of franchising and solopreneurship, stressing the differences in risk, investment, and control, and will guide you to the route that best matches your vision.

The advantages and disadvantages of franchising

Franchising is an appealing option for those who want to run a company but want the security of an established brand and structure. However, it is not without its drawbacks.

Pros of franchising:

1. Established Brand Recognition:

Franchise firms often have a devoted client base and a trustworthy reputation, removing the need to establish brand recognition from the beginning.

This advantage generally results in quicker income production than launching a new firm.

2. Proven business model:

Franchises follow tried-and-true procedures, providing operating parameters, marketing tactics, and product/service consistency.

These solutions drastically minimize the trial and error period of company ownership.

3. Support and training:

Franchisors often give initial and continuing training, marketing materials, and operational assistance to ensure franchisees are prepared for success.

Access to a network of other franchisees may provide guidance and friendship.

4. Easy Financing Options:

Banks and lenders may be more likely to fund a franchise because of its established track record and lower risk than a startup.

Cons of franchising:

1. Initial and ongoing costs:

Franchise fees and royalties may be large, reducing profitability.

Some franchises demand significant upfront expenditures in equipment, inventory, and marketing.

2. Limited Control:

Franchise agreements sometimes include tight branding, pricing, and operational guidelines, which restrict your creative flexibility. As a franchisee, you must follow the franchisor's procedures, even if you think that some adjustments might benefit your firm.

3. Potential for conflict:

Disagreements with the franchisor over fees, territorial rights, or operational changes may emerge.

Poor actions or controversies involving the franchisor may have a negative influence on your franchise location.

4. Shared reputation:

Your company's reputation is linked to the whole brand. If other franchisees perform badly or the franchisor receives criticism, your company may suffer as a result.

Pros and Cons of Solopreneurship

Solopreneurship gives you the maximum flexibility to build a firm that represents your unique vision. However, this independence comes with obstacles that need strength and resolve.

Advantages of Solopreneurship:

1. Complete creative freedom:

As a solopreneur, you have complete control over all aspects of your firm, from branding to operations.

You can quickly pivot to respond to market shifts or seize new possibilities.

2. Reduced initial costs:

Starting your firm usually needs less initial money than buying a franchise.

You may build your firm at your speed, reinvesting earnings as it grows.

3. Ownership of Success:

Every milestone you reach is the direct consequence of your hard work and inventiveness, which makes achievement very rewarding.

You keep 100% of the earnings, with no royalties or franchise fees to pay.

4. Personal Branding Opportunities:

Solopreneurs are allowed to create a personal brand that represents their beliefs and hobbies.

This link has the potential to increase market uniqueness and consumer loyalty.

Cons of solopreneurship:

1. Higher Risk and Uncertainty:

Without an established company plan, you must depend on your market research and intuition to succeed.

Financial risk is elevated, particularly in the early phases.

2. A steeper learning curve:

Solopreneurs must wear several hats, including marketing, operations, bookkeeping, and customer service.

If a support structure is not in place, burnout might occur.

3. Longer path to profitability: Building brand recognition and a consumer base takes time, particularly in highly competitive sectors.

Profitability might take months or even years to establish.

4. Isolation.

Operating a one-person company may be isolating, especially without a network of peers or mentors.

Decision-making may be difficult without a sounding board for ideas.

Key Differences in Risk, Investment, and Control

When deciding between franchising and solopreneurship, think about how each option fits with your risk tolerance, available resources, and desire for control.

Risk: Franchises often carry reduced risk owing to their existing brand and processes, but solopreneurship involves more risk since you are beginning from nothing.

Investment: Franchises often have greater upfront expenditures but predictable expenses. Solopreneurship offers you more flexibility in investing, but expenses might be unexpected.

Control: Franchising restricts creative freedom while providing structure. Solopreneurship provides complete control but requires self-discipline and decision-making abilities.

Evaluating Which Option Fits Your Lifestyle and Goals

To choose the best option for you, consider your personality, resources, and future goals.

Key Questions to Consider:

Do you like to follow established norms, or do you

value individuality and creativity?

Do you prefer the security of an established system, or are you ready to take the risks of starting from scratch?

What amount of financial and time investment are you willing to make?

How much say do you want in the branding, operations, and direction of your company?

Lifestyle considerations:

If you value work-life balance and like a structured setting, franchising might be a good match.

If you value flexibility and the ability to create, solopreneurship may be a better fit for you.

The Crossroads of Opportunity

Both franchising and solopreneurship provide excellent prospects for personal and professional development. Neither approach is intrinsically superior—it all depends on what aligns with your vision, values, and circumstances.

Understanding the advantages and drawbacks of each option, assessing your risk tolerance, and aligning your decision with your lifestyle and objectives can allow you to go on a journey that is both exciting and rewarding. The option is yours, and whichever route you choose, will be the first step toward the life you've always wanted.

Chapter 3: Market Research and Finding Your Niche

Behind every successful firm is a thorough grasp of its target market. Market research is the basis upon which great companies are founded, acting as a compass to direct your strategy, services, and growth.

Whether you're franchising or starting your firm as a solopreneur, establishing your expertise and catering to client demands is critical. This chapter delves into how to identify insights that can offer you a competitive advantage, assess industry trends, and perform successful market research using tools and methodologies.

Why Market Research Matters

Market research addresses the fundamental concerns that any entrepreneur must ask:

Who are my patrons?

What are their needs, wants, and values?

How can I provide a better solution than everyone else?

Without market research, you risk designing items or services that do not resonate with your target audience. Instead of guessing, research gives you clarity and confidence to make data-driven judgments.

Benefits of Market Research:
1. Identifies market opportunities and gaps.
2. Minimise risk by confirming concepts before launching.
3. Allows you to adapt your marketing and communication tactics.
4. Oversees price, positioning, and product development.
5. Keeps you updated on rivals and industry developments.

Understanding Your Target Market and Customer Needs.

Your target market is the group of individuals who are most likely to purchase your goods or services. Understanding their demographics, interests, and pain issues is the first step toward creating a company that serves them.

Steps for defining your target market:

1. Segment the market:
Divide the larger market into distinct segments based on demographics (age, gender, income), psychographics

(lifestyle, values, interests), and behavior (purchase habits, brand loyalty).

2. Create customer personas.

Create thorough profiles for your ideal consumers. For instance, "Sarah, 35, is a working mum who prioritizes convenience and sustainability." She's prepared to pay more for environmentally friendly things that save her time."

3. Identify customer needs and pain points:

What issues do your clients face?

How are they presently addressing these issues, and where do existing solutions fall short?

4. Concentrate on Value:

Customers care about how your product or service will benefit them. Highlight the benefits you provide, whether it is saving time, enhancing their life, or providing higher quality.

Evaluating Industry Trends and Opportunities

Every sector is influenced by changing trends and consumer behavior. Staying updated about these developments can help you position your company to capitalize on possibilities.

Where to Look for Industry Trends?

1. Industry Reports & Publications:

Subscribe to trade publications, market research studies, and industry newsletters to keep current.

2. Competitive Analysis:

Examine your rivals' strengths and weaknesses.

Determine trends in their products, pricing, and marketing techniques.

3. Social Media & Online Communities:

Twitter, Reddit, and LinkedIn are good sources for real-time information and new trends.

Keep an eye on industry-specific hashtags, forums, and organizations.

4. Economic and Technology Trends:

How do wider economic and technological trends affect your industry? For example, the growth of e-commerce and AI has transformed several sectors.

Finding Opportunities in the Market:

Search for untapped consumer niches or unmet demands.

Consider how you may innovate in your sector or mix trends in new ways.

Ask, "What's next?" Think ahead of the curve.

Tools and Methods for Effective Marketing Research

Market research does not have to be complicated or costly. With the correct tools and procedures, you can collect useful data without breaking the bank.

Primary Research: Collect information directly from your target audience.

1) Surveys and Questionnaires:

Create surveys using technologies such as Google Forms, SurveyMonkey, and Typeform.

Keep your inquiries basic and relevant to your aims, such as identifying preferences or assessing demand.

2. Interviews and focus groups:

Conduct one-on-one interviews or group conversations to learn about consumer attitudes and behaviors.

These approaches provide extensive, qualitative findings.

3. Customer Observations:

Visit businesses, events, or online platforms where your target audience engages. Pay attention to their actions, decisions, and complaints.

Secondary research involves using existing data from credible sources.

1. Market Research Reports.

Companies such as IBISWorld, Statista, and Nielsen provide thorough industry information (some may need a membership).

2. Governmental Data:

Websites such as the United States Census Bureau and Eurostat give free demographic and economic data.

3. Competitor Analysis Tools:

You may use tools like SEMrush and SimilarWeb to analyze your rivals' online performance.

Social Listening:

Use apps like Hootsuite, Brandwatch, or Sprout Social to track talks about your industry, rivals, or brand.

Search for repeating themes, complaints, or new requirements.

Experimentation & Test:

Start a modest pilot program or run advertisements to gauge interest in your product or service.

Use A/B testing to compare alternative marketing messages, designs, or features.

Finding and Owning Your Niche

Your niche is the exact segment of the market in which you thrive. Finding the correct specialty can help you stand out and establish a loyal consumer base.

How To Identify Your Niche:

1. Align Passions with Market Needs:

Where do your passions overlap with consumer demand?

2. Focus on Specialisation:

Instead of trying to please everyone, focus on one area where you can excel.

For example, rather than beginning a generic fitness

firm, concentrate on "fitness programs for new moms."

3. Stand out from competitors: What makes you unique? Your specialization might be a product characteristic, service quality, or personal brand.

4. Test and refine:

Begin with a clear understanding of your specialty, but be adaptable. Customer feedback and market changes may force you to modify your emphasis.

The Road Ahead

Effective market research and niche selection are continual operations that change with your firm. You can keep your firm current and competitive by constantly listening to your market, analyzing trends, and fine-tuning your strategy.

Remember, establishing your niche is more than simply spotting a market gap; it's about deciding where you can flourish, make a difference, and create something amazing. With a solid grasp of your target market and a clear focus, you're ready to take the next step in your entrepreneurial journey.

Chapter 4: Developing a Winning Business Plan

A business plan is more than a paper; it serves as the roadmap for your entrepreneurial journey. It turns your vision into tangible actions, offering a road map for expansion, directing decision-making, and acting as a compelling tool for obtaining finance. Whether you're establishing a franchise or beginning a company from scratch as a solopreneur, a good business plan is critical to success.

This chapter delves into the fundamental components of a successful business plan, such as developing a clear vision and purpose, defining realistic objectives and milestones, and mastering the art of financial planning.

Creating a clear vision and mission.

Your vision and purpose are the foundation of your company strategy. They clarify your mission, motivate action, and convey your goals to stakeholders.

1. Vision Statement: Your Dream Defined.

Your vision statement is your "why." It encapsulates the core of your long-term company goals. A great vision guides your staff, inspires them, and connects with consumers.

Key Questions for Developing Your Vision Statement:

What kind of influence do you hope your company will have?

How do you picture your company expanding and changing in five, 10, or twenty years?

What legacy do you want to leave behind?

Examples of powerful vision statements:

"To create a world where sustainable living is the norm."

"To be the leading provider of accessible and innovative fitness solutions for families worldwide."

2. Mission Statement: Your Purpose in Action.

Your vision is your goal, and your mission is the practical step toward realizing that ambition. It defines your company's mission, target audience, and unique value offer.

Key elements of a mission statement:

Purpose: Why does your company exist?

Who is your target audience?

Value Proposition: What differentiates you from competitors?

Example of a Mission Statement: "Our goal is to provide healthy, convenient meal options for busy professionals that save time and promote well-being."

Setting realistic goals and milestones.

A solid business plan contains specific objectives and milestones that translate your vision into actionable activities. These objectives should be specified, measurable, achievable, relevant, and time-bound (SMART).

1. divide Down Your Goals: Identify your main goals and divide them down into smaller, manageable stages.

Example Goals:

Short-term: Launch your website within three months.

Medium-Term Goal: Generate $50,000 in income during the first year.

Long-term: Open a second site within five years.

2. Set Milestones: Milestones are milestones to measure progress and stay focused.

Examples of Milestones:

Secure your first hundred consumers.

Hire your first employee.

Achieve profitability.

3. Be Flexible: While goals give guidance, flexibility is essential. Market factors, client feedback, and unexpected problems may force you to change your strategy. Regularly examine and update your objectives to ensure they are still relevant.

Financial planning includes budgeting, forecasting, and securing funding.

Financial planning is a crucial component of any business strategy. Investors, lenders, and even your staff want assurance that your company is financially viable.

1. Budgeting: Planning Your Expenses and Revenues

A thorough budget allows you to properly manage resources and minimize overpaying.

Key components of a budget:

Startup costs include equipment, licensing, legal expenses, initial inventory, and marketing.

Operating costs include rent, utilities, payroll, supplies, and insurance.

Revenue projections are estimated earnings from sales, services, or other sources.

Tips For Effective Budgeting:

Be cautious with income projections and realistic with spending.

Include reserve money for unforeseen expenses.

Track and manage your budget using software such as QuickBooks or Excel.

2. Forecasting: Estimating Future Performance

Financial forecasting involves predicting your revenue, costs, and profitability over time. This is crucial for making decisions and recruiting investment.

How to make a financial forecast:

Analyse industry benchmarks to forecast revenue growth.

Consider seasonal patterns and economic situations.

Use historical data (if available) or market-based assumptions.

Key Financial Projections to Include:

Profit and Loss Statement (Income Statement): Displays revenue, expenses, and profits for a specified period.

The fund's Flow Statement tracks the input and outflow of funds to guarantee liquidity.

The balance sheet summarises your assets, liabilities, and equity.

3. Getting Funding: Financing Your Vision

If your company wants external finance, your

business plan must illustrate why it is a good investment.

Funding Options:

Personal Savings: Self-financing is a popular beginning point for many enterprises.

Loans: Traditional bank loans or small business loans (such as SBA loans).

Investors include angel investors, venture capitalists, and crowdsourcing sites such as Kickstarter.

Franchise-Specific Financing: Many franchisors provide in-house financing or collaborate with lenders.

Investors and lenders look for:

A clear and appealing business concept.

Strong financial expectations and a balanced budget.

Proof of market demand and a competitive edge.

Writing a funding proposal:

Include an executive summary, company description, financial predictions, and a fundraising request.

Highlight how the cash will be used and the possible return on investment.

Bring It All Together

A successful business plan is more than statistics and assertions; it tells the tale of your vision, strategy, and potential. It's a live document that changes as your company develops, allowing you to remain focused, react to problems, and grasp opportunities.

Make your strategy clear, simple, and motivating, whether you're presenting it to investors, discussing it with your team, or following it as a personal guide. Your business plan is more than simply a paper; it's the link between your vision and reality.

You may prepare for long-term success by creating a clear vision, setting realistic objectives, and establishing a strong financial basis. With your strategy in hand, you can confidently and move forward in your business path.

Chapter 5: Navigating Franchising: What to Look For

Franchising may be an effective approach to joining the world of company ownership by leveraging an existing brand and proven procedures. However, not all franchises are created equal, and your choices from the start might decide whether your company succeeds or fails. To succeed in franchising, you must first comprehend franchise agreements and fees, then study and choose the best franchise, and develop good connections with franchisors and other franchise owners.

This chapter is your full guide to franchising, allowing you to make educated choices and position yourself for long-term success.

Understand Franchise Agreements and Fees

The franchise agreement is at the core of every franchising opportunity since it outlines the relationship between you (the franchisee) and the franchisor. It is critical to understand the terms of this agreement since they regulate everything from your rights and duties to the charges involved.

1. What is a Franchise Agreement?

A franchise agreement is a binding legal contract that details:

The scope and duration of your franchise ownership.

Your duties include branding, operations, and reporting.

The franchisor's obligations include training, support, and marketing.

Because this agreement is legally binding, it is critical to carefully examine it and speak with a franchise attorney before signing.

2. Key Elements of a Franchise Agreement:

Initial Franchise cost: A one-time cost paid to the franchisor for the opportunity to operate under their name.

Royalty Fees: Ongoing payments (often a percentage of your earnings) that help finance the franchisor's support services.

Advertising fees are contributions to the franchisor's marketing and advertising activities.

Territory Rights: The geographical region in which you may run your franchise.

Termination Clauses: The terms under which any party may terminate the agreement.

3. Questions About Fees and Agreements:

What's included in the first franchise fee?

Are royalty payments calculated based on gross sales or net profit?

How are advertising costs spent, and do they help my location?

What are the renewal provisions of the franchise agreement?

Understanding this information allows you to determine if the franchise opportunity is compatible with your financial objectives and operational preferences.

Researching and Selecting the Right Franchise

Choosing the appropriate franchise is one of the most important choices you can make as an entrepreneur. The most suitable franchise for you is determined by your hobbies, talents, financial resources, and market demand.

1. Begin with Self-Reflection: Before exploring franchise options, ask yourself:

What industries fascinate me?

What are my talents and abilities, and how may they help me succeed?

What amount of investment do I feel comfortable with?

Do I prefer a hands-on job or supervising operations?

2. Explore Franchise Opportunities: There are several franchise opportunities available, from food and retail to health services and education. To limit your options, consider:

Industry Trends: Look for sectors that are growing and in great demand.

Reputation: Look at the franchisor's track record, customer happiness, and feedback from existing franchisees.

Scalability: Does the franchise have the potential to develop and expand?

3. Conduct Due Diligence: Proper research is crucial to prevent expensive blunders. Key steps include:

Reviewing the Franchise Disclosure Document (FDD): This document offers specific information on the franchisor, including fees, duties, and performance indicators.

Analysing Financials: Determine the franchise's profitability and the normal period to return your investment.

Speaking with Existing Franchisees: Enquire about their experiences, issues, and general satisfaction with the franchiser's assistance.

4. Red Flags to Watch Out For:
Uncertain or high fees.

High franchisee turnover rate.

The franchisor provides little assistance and training.

Lack of openness in financial reporting.

Developing relationships with franchisors and franchisees.

The success of your franchise is determined not only by the brand but also by the connections you establish inside the franchise network. Building excellent relationships with the franchisor and other franchisees may give invaluable insights, support, and chances for cooperation.

1. Establishing Trust and Communication with the Franchisor: As a business partner, it's important to build a relationship with the franchisor.

Tips for Developing Positive Relationships:

Ask questions: Demonstrate a genuine interest in knowing their vision, goals, and support systems.

Be proactive: Take use of the franchisor's training programs, resources, and tools.

Provide Feedback: Share your experiences and recommendations for improvement; constructive feedback helps the whole franchise network.

What to Look for in a Franchisor?

A dedication to franchisee success.

Transparency and response.

A demonstrated history of innovation and adaptation.

2. Networking with other franchisees may provide useful information and assistance. Their direct knowledge may assist you in navigating hurdles, avoiding mistakes, and maximizing possibilities.

Ways to Connect with Franchisees:

Attend Franchise Meetings and Events: Several franchisors host yearly conferences or regional meetings.

Join Online Forums and Groups: Platforms like Facebook and LinkedIn often feature franchise-specific forums.

Collaborate Locally: Form partnerships with franchisees in your area to share marketing resources or information.

Advantages of a Strong Franchise Network:

Gain access to shared best practices and solutions.

Emotional assistance at difficult times.

Opportunities to work together on collective efforts like regional marketing or bulk buying.

The Power of Making an Informed Decision

Navigating franchising requires effort, curiosity, and a dedication to comprehending the complexities of the system. By meticulously analyzing franchise agreements and fees, performing extensive research, and building genuine connections, you may create the groundwork for a successful franchise enterprise.

Remember that the appropriate franchise is one that reflects your beliefs, interests, and aspirations. It's more than simply a business choice; it's a collaboration that should help you succeed as an entrepreneur. With careful preparation and educated decisions, you may boldly enter the world of franchising and begin creating the future you choose.

Chapter 6: The Solopreneur Mindset: Building from the Ground Up

Choosing to become a solopreneur is both inspiring and hard. Unlike franchising, where procedures are set for you, solopreneurs build everything from the ground up—your brand, operations, and the core of your company identity. Success as a solopreneur involves not just strategic preparation, but also a resilient attitude that values independence, inventiveness, and flexibility.

This chapter delves into the fundamental components of the solopreneur attitude, including defining a brand and value proposition, constructing an operational strategy, and balancing independence with significant support networks.

Building a Brand and Value Proposition

Your brand is more than just a logo or slogan; it represents the core of your company and how people perceive it. A great brand distinguishes you from the competition, fosters trust, and effectively conveys your unique value offer.

1. Developing your brand identity

To build a distinctive and genuine brand, begin by identifying the essential values and vision that guide your company.

Key Questions for Defining Your Brand:

What are your company's key values?

What feelings or thoughts do you hope your brand would evoke?

How would you want consumers to describe your company to others?

Characteristics of a Strong Brand Identity:

Logo and Visual Design: Select colors, typefaces, and pictures that express your brand's personality.

Voice and Tone: Determine how your brand "speaks," whether it is professional, welcoming, or fun.

Brand Story: Tell us about your journey, purpose, and what makes your company distinctive.

For example, a sustainable skincare company may emphasize eco-conscious principles, employ earth-toned designs, and communicate in a pleasant and instructive manner.

2. Develop Your Value Proposition.

Your value proposition is the promise of the advantages that clients will get if they choose your firm. It is the response to the inquiry, "Why should I buy from you instead of someone else?"

Steps for creating a compelling value proposition:

Determine your target audience's major pain areas.

Explain how your product or service outperforms the competition in addressing those issues.

Highlight the distinct characteristics or advantages you provide.

Like this one: "Our all-natural skincare line provides

effective, chemical-free solutions for sensitive skin, ensuring health and peace of mind for environmentally conscious consumers."

Developing a Solid Operational Plan

An operational strategy is the foundation of your solopreneur firm. It guarantees that your whole operation, from manufacturing to customer service, operates smoothly and effectively.

1. Establishing Your Operations: As a solopreneur, you may need to take on many roles, such as marketing and accounting. Streamlining your processes is critical to increasing productivity.

Key areas to address:

Production: How will you manufacture or get your goods or services?

How will you provide your goods or services to customers?

Customer Support: How will you manage inquiries, comments, and issues?

Tools & Resources:

Organise tasks using project management software such as Trello or Asana.

To better manage your funds, consider investing in accounting software such as QuickBooks.

Use Zapier or Hootsuite to automate monotonous chores.

2. Plan for Growth: Consider scalability, even when beginning small. How can you expand your company without overloading yourself?

Tips for Scalable Operations:

Create systems and procedures that are readily copied.

As your firm expands, outsource non-core duties (for example, accounting and graphic design).

Investigate technologies that may save time, such as e-commerce platforms or chatbots.

Balancing Independence and Support Networks.

One of the most appealing aspects of solopreneurship is independence—you have complete control over your firm. However, functioning solo does not imply that you must do everything alone. Creating and relying on support networks may help you overcome obstacles, get fresh insights, and remain motivated.

1. The Importance of Support Networks:

A robust support network provides:

Emotional support: Other entrepreneurs understand the ups and downs of operating a company.

Practical Advice: Learn from other people's experiences, faults, and accomplishments.

Opportunities: Networking may lead to collaborations,

recommendations, and career advancement.

2. Types of Support Networks:
Professional Communities: Participate in local business organizations, industry associations, or internet forums.

Mentors: Find experienced entrepreneurs who can provide advice and accountability.

Friends and family: They may not grasp every aspect of your company, but their encouragement and support are vital.

3. Recognising the Need for Outside Expertise: While independence is a strength, it's crucial to recognize when it's time to seek help. When confronted with issues outside of your comfort zone, don't be afraid to engage a consultant, enroll in a course, or seek guidance.

The Solopreneur Mindset: Thrive on Your Terms

Embracing the solopreneur attitude entails accepting responsibility for your success while staying open to learning, development, and cooperation. It's about creating a company that is consistent with your vision and beliefs, fuelled by your creativity and dedication.

You'll set yourself up for long-term success by building a strong brand, creating a clear value offer, optimizing your processes, and surrounding yourself with supporting networks. Solopreneurship may be a lonely road, but with the correct mentality and techniques, it may lead to boundless possibilities and personal fulfillment.

Chapter 7: Essential Tools and

Resources for Entrepreneurs

Entrepreneurship demands not just passion and vision, but also the necessary tools and resources to turn your ideas into a profitable firm. From cutting-edge technology to meaningful mentorships and active online platforms, arming yourself with the appropriate tools may help you optimize operations, broaden your reach, and accelerate your development. This chapter will look at three important pillars of entrepreneurial success: using technology and software, capitalizing on networking and mentoring opportunities, and using online platforms for marketing and sales.

Technology and Software for Streamlined Operations

In today's fast-paced business environment, technology is

your greatest friend. The correct software and solutions may automate activities, increase productivity, and free up your time to concentrate on strategic development.

1. Tools for organization and productivity

Any business must be able to stay organized and manage their time properly. These tools may assist.

Trello and Asana are visual project management software that helps you monitor projects, deadlines, and progress.

Google Workspace is a collection of applications (Docs, Sheets, Drive, and Gmail) for collaboration, document sharing, and communication.

Notion: A customizable platform for managing notes, tasks, and projects.

2. Financial Management Software.

Understanding your company's financial situation is critical. These tools streamline accounting, invoicing, and budgeting:

QuickBooks is a complete accounting application for small companies.

Wave is a free solution for invoicing and bookkeeping.

Expensify simplifies expenditure monitoring and reimbursements.

3. Marketing and Social Media Tools.

Effective marketing is essential for reaching your intended audience. Utilize these platforms to strengthen your efforts.

Canva: An easy-to-use design tool for making social media posts, flyers, and commercials.

Hootsuite/Buffer: Schedule and manage postings on several social media networks.

Mailchimp is an email marketing tool for creating and

maintaining consumer connections.

4. E-commerce and Payment Processing.

These systems make transactions smooth for those offering items or services online.

Shopify is a popular platform for creating and managing online shops.

Stripe provides secure payment processing for online commerce.

Square combines in-person and online payment options.

5. Customer Relationship Management (CRM).

Building and sustaining client connections is critical to long-term success.

HubSpot CRM is a free and effective solution for monitoring customer interactions.

Salesforce is a comprehensive CRM system designed for bigger, developing enterprises.

Zoho CRM is an affordable and scalable CRM solution for small and medium-sized organizations.

Networking and Mentoring Opportunities

As an entrepreneur, your network is one of your most precious assets. Building connections with mentors, peers, and industry experts may give you insights, support, and opportunities that you would not have discovered on your own.

1. The Power of Networking.

Networking is more than simply passing business cards; it is about making genuine contacts that promote mutual progress.

Attend Local Events: Business meetings, conferences, and trade exhibits are fantastic opportunities to meet like-minded people.

Join Professional Groups: Organisations such as BNI (Business Network

International) and Chamber of Commerce chapters provide networking possibilities.

Online Communities: LinkedIn, Reddit, and Facebook groups let you connect with experts in your sector.

2. Finding the Right Mentors.

A mentor may be a source of inspiration, providing guidance, sharing experiences, and assisting you in overcoming obstacles.

Where to find mentors:

SCORE provides free mentoring services to seasoned business professionals.

Industry Events: Many successful businesses welcome mentoring possibilities.

Alumni Networks: Connect with accomplished alumni of your institution or university.

What to look for in a mentor.

Industry expertise that is relevant to your company.

A readiness to provide honest comments.

Consistent with your principles and ambitions.

3. Peer Support

Fellow entrepreneurs at a comparable stage may often give the most relevant advice and support.

Mastermind groups are small groups of entrepreneurs that meet regularly to provide ideas and assistance.

Incubators and accelerators are programs that give resources, money, and mentoring to companies.

Coworking spaces are ideal for meeting local businesses and encouraging cooperation.

Leveraging Online Platforms for Marketing and Sales

In today's digital world, a good online presence is critical to attracting and maintaining clients. Online platforms provide limitless opportunities for marketing, sales, and consumer involvement.

1. Create a website.

Customers' initial engagement with your brand is frequently via your website. It should be professional, user-friendly, and consistent with your brand.

Platforms for creating websites:

WordPress is a versatile and powerful website builder.

Squarespace and Wix are user-friendly tools for building beautiful, customizable websites.

Shopify is ideal for e-commerce firms.

Essential Elements of a Website:

Simple navigation and layout.

Mobile responsiveness.

Engaging material that articulates your value offer.

2. Social Media Marketing.

Social media platforms enable you to engage with your target audience, tell your narrative, and market your goods or services.

Selecting the Right Platform:
Instagram provides visual storytelling for lifestyle, fashion, and culinary companies.
LinkedIn: Professional networking for B2B businesses.
TikTok: A short-form video platform for younger audiences.
Content Strategy:
Share behind-the-scenes information to increase authenticity.
Engage your fans with surveys, Q&A sessions, and comments.
Use user-generated material to demonstrate client pleasure.
3. Online advertising.
Paid advertising may help you expand your reach and increase traffic to your website or business.
Google Ads: Find consumers who are actively looking for items or services similar to yours.

Facebook advertising: Highly customizable advertising with advanced targeting capabilities.

Influencer Marketing: Collaborate with influencers to reach their devoted audience.

4. Email Marketing.

Email is one of the most successful methods for nurturing leads and maintaining client connections.

Create an email list: Provide significant incentives, such as discounts or free materials, in return for email signups.

Segment your audience and send personalized emails based on their behavior and interests.

Measure performance by tracking open rates, click-through rates, and conversions.

Bring It All Together

Equipping yourself with the correct tools, resources, and contacts will help you grow your company from a concept to a profitable organization. You will prepare your firm for long-term development and success by simplifying operations using technology, cultivating partnerships via networking and mentoring, and exploiting online platforms for marketing and sales.

Remember that entrepreneurship isn't about doing everything on your own; it's about knowing where to locate the necessary resources and tools to help you realize your idea. With these resources, you're not simply operating a company; you're creating a future.

Chapter 8: Legal, Financial, and

Administrative Essentials

Starting a company is an exhilarating experience, but it also comes with a slew of legal, financial, and administrative responsibilities that may be daunting. While the creative and operational parts of company ownership are often highlighted, building a solid foundation in these areas is critical to avoiding expensive errors and ensuring long-term success.

This chapter will walk you through the elements of establishing your business structure, comprehending tax duties and accounting fundamentals, and safeguarding your company with insurance and legal precautions. Each phase will help you strengthen your company's foundation, providing you the confidence to concentrate on development and innovation.

Setting up Your Business Structure

Choosing the appropriate legal form for your company is one of the most important choices you will make. Your company structure has an impact on everything from taxes and liabilities to capital raising and operational management.

1. Types of Business Structures

Sole Proprietorship is a basic form suitable for small businesses.

Pros: Simple to set up, minimal cost, total control.

Cons: There is no separation of personal and corporate liabilities.

Partnership: A firm owned by two or more people.

Advantages: Shared duty and resources.

Cons: Personal accountability for all partners; conflicts may disrupt business.

A Limited Liability Company (LLC) offers the freedom of a single proprietorship while providing liability protection similar to a corporation.

Pros: Personal assets are safeguarded, and there are numerous tax alternatives.

Cons: There may be greater costs and more paperwork than with a single proprietorship.

Corporations (C Corp or S Corp) are a more complicated form suitable for enterprises seeking to raise large cash.

Pros: Limited liability makes it simpler to recruit investors.

Cons: More restrictions and double taxes for C corporations unless they are formed as S corporations.

2. Factors to Consider When Selecting a Structure:

Liability Protection: Is it necessary to separate personal and corporate assets?

Tax Implications: How will the structure influence your tax obligations?

Scalability: Is the structure appropriate for expansion or future investment?

Administrative burden: Can you handle the paperwork and regulatory requirements?

3. How to Set Up Your Business Structure:

Register your company name with the state or municipal authorities.

Fill out the necessary documentation (such as Articles of Organisation for an LLC).

Get an Employer Identification Number (EIN) from the IRS.

Meet any further state or local licensing requirements.

Understanding Tax Obligations and Accounting Basics

Taxes and accounting may not be the most attractive components of an enterprise, but they are among the most crucial. Proper management of these areas assures compliance and provides you with a comprehensive view of your company's financial situation.

1. Understanding Your Tax Obligations.

Your tax obligations vary depending on the form of your firm, its location, and sector.

Income tax is levied on your earnings. Sole owners record company revenue on their tax returns, while corporations do so separately.

Self-employment tax: Includes Social Security and Medicare payments.

Sales tax is required for firms that sell physical items or certain services, depending on state legislation.

Employment Taxes: If you hire people, you must withhold income taxes and pay Social Security and Medicare taxes.

2. Tools and Strategies for Tax Simplification:

Keep track of your revenue and spending with accounting software such as QuickBooks or FreshBooks.

Create a second company bank account to keep your funds organized.

Hire a tax expert to guarantee compliance and take advantage of deductions.

3. Accounting Basics for Entrepreneurs

Even if you employ an accountant, knowing the fundamentals of accounting is critical.

Key Financial Statements:

Profit and Loss Statement: A record of income, costs, and earnings over a certain period.

The balance sheet summarises assets, liabilities, and equity.

Funds Flow Statement: Displays the flow of funds into and out of your firm.

Tips For Effective Bookkeeping:

Keep quick records of all financial transactions.

To minimize surprises, monitor cash flow regularly.

Reconcile your accounts once a month to spot problems early.

Protecting Your Business with Insurance and Legal Guards

Even if you properly prepare, unforeseen circumstances might ruin your company. Insurance and legal protections are vital for reducing risk and protecting your hard work.

1. Types of Business Insurance

General liability insurance covers claims involving accidents, injuries, or property damage.

Professional Liability Insurance: Covers allegations of carelessness or errors in your services.

Product Liability Insurance: Required if your company makes or sells items.

Property insurance covers the damage or loss of commercial property caused by catastrophes such as fires or theft.

Workers' Compensation Insurance is required if you have workers and covers injuries received on the job.

2. Legal safeguards.

Contracts: Use unambiguous, written agreements for all company transactions, including vendor partnerships and client interactions.

Trademarks: Protect your company's name, logo, and other branding features to prevent others from using them.

Non-disclosure agreements (NDAs): Protect sensitive information while dealing with contractors or colleagues.

Compliance: Stay up to speed on industry-specific rules and regulations, such as data privacy and employment legislation.

3. Create a Risk Management Plan

Identify Potential hazards: Think about hazards unique to your sector, such as cyberattacks or supply chain disruptions.

Mitigate hazards: Create ways to lessen the probability or severity of certain hazards.

Prepare for Emergencies: Have a strategy in place to deal with big interruptions like natural catastrophes or economic downturns.

Foundation of a Secure Business

The legal, financial, and administrative components of entrepreneurship may seem overwhelming, yet they form the foundation of a successful and long-lasting firm. By establishing the proper structure, keeping on top of taxes and accounting, and proactively defending your firm, you can concentrate on what is important: expanding and thriving as an entrepreneur.

Remember that starting a company is more than simply following your passion; it's also about ensuring that your hard work is protected and complies with the rules and regulations that govern it. Taking the effort to address these critical issues now will save you problems in the future and position you for long-term success.

Chapter 9: Building a Team and Scaling Your Business

As your firm expands, the demands on your time and energy will surely rise. At some point, it is impossible to accomplish everything by oneself. That is when assembling a team and expanding your business comes into play. This chapter will walk you through the basic procedures of recruiting and managing staff or contractors, developing a strong corporate culture, and preparing for long-term development.

Whether you're employing your first employee or growing into a bigger organization, the choices you make today will set the stage for your company's long-term success.

Hiring and Managing Employees and Contractors

Hiring the appropriate personnel is one of the most important aspects of growing your company. The people you hire will have a huge impact on the direction of your organization.

1. Identifying your needs.

Before recruiting, examine your company processes and identify areas where extra assistance is most required.

What are the most time-consuming chores for you?

Are there any specialized talents that might enhance your offerings?

Are you looking for full-time employees, part-time workers, or contractors?

2. Crafting Job Descriptions

A concise and interesting job description attracts qualified applicants. Include:

Role Overview: What does the role comprise and how does it tie into the overall aims of your company?

Key responsibilities include specific activities and objectives.

Required Skills and Experience: Non-negotiable credentials, as well as desirable characteristics.

Company Culture: A concise summary of your values and work environment.

3. Recruitment and Interviewing

Finding the proper personnel requires more than just

reading resumes. Use many avenues to discover talent:

Job boards include platforms like Indeed, LinkedIn, and Glassdoor.

Referrals: Ask current workers or professional contacts to propose applicants.

Freelance platforms, such as Upwork or Fiverr, are used for short-term or specialized assignments.

Interview tips:

Ask behavioral questions (e.g., "Tell me about a time you overcame a challenge at work").

Assess both cultural fit and technical skills.

Provide realistic tasks or assessments to assess real-world performance.

4. Managing your team

Once you've recruited your staff, good management is critical to sustaining productivity and morale.

Set clear expectations: Offer precise onboarding and clear objectives.

Communication: Encourage open and frequent communication via team meetings and one-on-one conversations.

Comments and Growth: Provide constructive comments and chances for professional growth.

5. Understanding Legal and Administrative Requirements

Hiring workers entails extra obligations, including:

Payroll and Benefits: To effectively handle payroll and benefits, use platforms such as Gusto or ADP.

Legal compliance entails adhering to labor rules such as contracts, taxes, and workplace safety.

Employee Handbooks: Create a handbook explaining the company's rules, procedures, and expectations.

Establishing a Company Culture and Leadership Style

The culture and leadership style you build will have an impact on your team's productivity, job happiness, and loyalty. A good corporate culture may also help you improve your reputation by recruiting top personnel and loyal consumers.

1. Define Your Company Culture

Company culture refers to the common beliefs, attitudes, and practices that define your organization.

Start with your values. Determine the basic values that govern your firm.

Involve Your Team: Encourage workers to share suggestions for creating a good workplace.

Living Your Culture: Leadership should demonstrate the behaviors and attitudes you wish to see.

2. Leadership Styles and their Impact

Your leadership style will determine how your team performs and develops. Common styles include:

Transformational leadership inspires creativity and motivates workers to achieve their full potential.

Servant leadership focuses on satisfying the needs of the team to enable them to achieve.

Authoritarian leadership sets clear goals and expectations, which is important in high-stakes circumstances.

3. Creating A Motivated Team

Recognition and Rewards: Recognise accomplishments with incentives, bonuses, or public acknowledgment.

Professional Development: Provide training, courses, and mentoring opportunities.

Work-Life Balance: Promote flexibility and support for personal well-being.

Planning for Growth and Scaling Operations Effectively

Scaling a firm entails more than just generating income; it requires a systematic strategy to expand operations, infrastructure, and market share.

1. Assessing Your Readiness to Scale

Before growing, make sure your firm is prepared for expansion by evaluating:

Market Demand: Is there an increasing demand for your product or service?

Financial Stability: Do you have the resources to sustain growth?

Operational Efficiency: Can your existing systems manage greater volume?

2. Create a Growth Strategy.

Scaling should follow a well-thought-out plan:

Set specific goals. Define growth in terms of revenue objectives, market share, or product lines.

Consider expanding your offerings by providing additional items or services.

Enter New Markets: Look for ways to broaden your reach geographically or demographically.

3. Automating and streamlining operations.

Efficiency is critical in handling growing demand:

Technology: Implement CRM systems, inventory management software, and AI-powered customer service.

Processes: Standardise procedures to ensure quality and consistency.

Outsourcing: Delegate non-core operations to third-party providers, such as IT support or logistics.

4. Managing finances During Growth

Scaling frequently requires substantial investment. Plan your money properly.

Loans, venture money, and crowdsourcing are all potential financing sources.

Cash Flow Management: Keep track of your revenue and spending to minimize liquidity concerns.

Budgeting for Growth: Set aside cash for marketing, recruiting, and infrastructure improvements.

5. Monitoring and Adjusting.

Growth is seldom linear, and setbacks are unavoidable. Maintain agility by:

Regularly monitoring performance indicators to discover opportunities for improvement.

Listening to consumer input to improve goods or services.

Being willing to pivot if a plan isn't producing results.

The Foundation for Long-Term Success

Building a team and expanding your company are transformational steps that need careful preparation and execution. By recruiting and managing the appropriate people, establishing a lively corporate culture, and intelligently growing operations, you may position your firm for long-term success.

Remember that growth is more than simply increasing your bottom line; it's about building a firm that is robust, inventive, and long-lasting. With the proper team and a sound strategy, the sky's the limit for what you can accomplish.

Chapter 10: Staying Inspired: Long-Term Success and Fulfillment

Creating a company is a marathon, not a sprint. While the early phases of entrepreneurship are fuelled by enthusiasm and passion, retaining that motivation in the long run may be difficult. Success requires more than simply hard effort; it also necessitates resilience, balance, and a strong sense of purpose.

In this chapter, we'll look at how to remain motivated throughout your entrepreneurial path, adapt to problems with grit and persistence, maintain a good work-life balance, and achieve fulfillment by utilizing your success to elevate and inspire others. True success is more than simply meeting financial objectives; it's about finding pleasure and purpose in the process and leaving a great legacy.

Adapting to challenges and being resilient

No entrepreneur's path is without challenges. From market downturns to personal failures, the capacity to adapt and persevere in the face of adversity is typically the determining factor in long-term success.

1. Adopting a growth mindset.

Resilience begins with thinking. A growth mentality, which believes that problems are chances for learning, may turn failures into stepping stones.

View Failure as Feedback: Every mistake teaches us something. Determine what went wrong and utilize it to improve.

Stay Curious: Always seek new information and abilities to adapt to changing conditions.

Be optimistic: Concentrate on what you can manage and have a positive outlook on the future.

2. Improving Problem-Solving Skills.

When faced with a task, critical and creative thinking skills are required.

Break down problems: Determine the fundamental cause of an issue and address it methodically.

Stay Calm Under Pressure: Use mindfulness methods to manage stress and think rationally.

Use Your Network: Get advice or solutions from mentors, peers, or your team.

3. Create a Support System

Resilience is seldom achieved alone by one person. Surrounding oneself with sympathetic people may assist you through difficult times.

Mentors and coaches: Their expertise and perspectives may help you navigate obstacles.

Peers and communities: Other entrepreneurs may provide encouragement and practical help.

Personal Support: Turn to family and friends for emotional support during tough times.

Maintaining Work-Life Balance and Preventing Burnout

Entrepreneurship often requires long hours and unwavering commitment, but ignoring your well-being may lead to burnout—a condition of physical and mental tiredness that can stymie your growth. Finding balance is not a luxury; it is a need.

1. Setting boundaries

Set clear boundaries between work and personal life to safeguard your time and energy.

Define Work Hours: Follow a timetable and prevent overextending yourself.

To psychologically disengage, create a workspace that is separate from your home place.

Learn to Say No: Turn down chances or responsibilities that don't fit with your aims or ideals.

2. Prioritising self-care.

Your health and well-being are the basis for your success.

Physical Health: Incorporate regular exercise, a good diet, and enough sleep into your daily routine.

Mental Health: Use mindfulness, meditation, or journaling to reduce stress.

Take pauses: Short pauses throughout the day, as well as extended vacations, will help you regain energy.

3. Delegation and Outsourcing

As your firm expands, attempting to handle everything alone may lead to fatigue.

Delegate tasks to your team, allowing you to concentrate on strategic choices.

Outsource Non-Core Activities: Hire freelancers or agencies to handle responsibilities like accountancy, marketing, and IT support.

Automate Repetitive Processes: Use technology to

improve efficiency and minimize effort.

4. Redefining Success.

To achieve balance, you must redefine your definition of success.

Beyond Money: Relationships, personal development, and influence are as important as financial gain.

Celebrate Small Wins: Recognise and praise progress, not just final objectives.

Stay True to Your Vision: To make your company more meaningful, align it with your interests and ideals.

Giving back: Using your success to inspire others.

True satisfaction frequently comes from sharing your achievements and assisting others on their path. Giving back not only enhances your life, but it also has a positive ripple impact in your neighborhood and beyond.

1. Mentoring aspiring entrepreneurs.

Your experiences, including achievements and mistakes, may be very beneficial to others.

Provide Guidance: Share your experiences via seminars, one-on-one mentorship, and public speaking.

Be Transparent: Discuss the difficulties you encountered and how you overcame them to encourage resilience.

Encourage collaboration by creating networks and groups to support the next generation of entrepreneurs.

2. Supporting Social Causes.

Use your platform and resources to change the world.

Corporate Social Responsibility (CSR): Build charity into your company model by contributing a share of revenues or volunteering as a group.

Sustainability Efforts: Reduce your environmental effects by adopting eco-friendly methods.

Community Engagement: Contribute to local projects, charities, or educational programs.

3. Building a Legacy

Think beyond the present and consider the long-term consequences of your job.

Create a Values-Driven Brand: Use your beliefs to influence your company choices and inspire others.

Empower Your Team: Create a culture of innovation and compassion that endures beyond your leadership.

Document Your Journey: Share your journey in books, blogs, or podcasts to provide a road map for future entrepreneurs.

Finding joy in the journey

Staying motivated as an entrepreneur is much more than just conquering obstacles and reaching milestones; it's about finding pleasure in the process. Celebrate the freedom to follow your aspirations, the connections you make along the road, and the chance to create something worthwhile.

Remember that success is a continuous path of development, discovery, and contribution. By remaining resilient, keeping balance, and giving back, you will not only find long-term fulfillment but also encourage others to pursue their aspirations and make a difference in the world. You can mold your life, company, and legacy, so think big, remain motivated, and never stop striving for the skies.

Conclusion: The Path to Business Ownership

Starting your own company is one of the most transforming and gratifying choices you can make. Whether you pick the controlled road of franchising or the autonomous route of solopreneurship, the entrepreneurial journey allows you to make your idea a reality, create something significant, and determine your future. This book has walked you through the key processes, difficulties, and benefits of establishing and running a successful company, providing inspiration, direction, and useful tools along the way.

Reflecting on the journey.

Every entrepreneur begins with a dream: a vision for a

better future. However, turning that concept into a successful company needs more than just desire. It requires meticulous preparation, unwavering dedication, and a readiness to adapt.

1. From Vision to Reality.

This tutorial has shown you how to:

Discover Your Purpose: By understanding your motivations and connecting your hobbies to a company concept, you've established the framework for a rewarding enterprise.

Navigate your options: Choosing between franchising and solopreneurship involves reflection, study, and a thorough grasp of your objectives, lifestyle, and risk tolerance.

2. Preparing Yourself for Success

With useful tools and methods, you've learned how to:

Conduct rigorous market research to identify your specialty.

Create a successful company strategy that acts as a road map for expansion.

Use technology, networks, and mentoring to solve problems.

3. Overcoming Challenges

Entrepreneurship is not without its challenges, but each one provides a chance to become stronger and wiser. You can weather any storm and emerge stronger by adopting a resilient mentality, creating equilibrium, and establishing a strong support system.

Your Position as a Leader and Creator

As a company owner, you're more than just an entrepreneur; you're also a leader, creator, and problem solver. Your efforts have an effect not just on your own life, but also on your colleagues, customers, and the community.

1. The Ripple Effect of Your Business

Every choice you make has a bigger impact:

Creating Jobs: By employing workers or working with contractors, you contribute to the economy.

Customer Service: Your goods or services help people solve issues, satisfy their needs, and live better lives.

Inspiring Others: Your story may inspire others to follow their aspirations and take charge of their destinies.

2. Establishing a Lasting Legacy

The company you create reflects your beliefs and ambitions. By adhering to your ideals and always striving for greatness, you leave a legacy that goes well beyond financial achievement.

The future is yours.

As you embark on your entrepreneurial journey, keep in mind that it will be a twisting route filled with learning, development, and change. Victories will confirm your purpose, and setbacks will test your determination, but each step will get you closer to realizing your goals.

1. Stay inspired.

Maintain focus on your "why" throughout your trip. Your mission, whether it be financial independence, artistic freedom, or making a difference in the world, will guide you through both trials and victories.

2. Embrace lifelong learning

The business environment is continuously changing, and being adaptive is critical to long-term success. Seek new information, welcome innovation, and be open to change.

3. Give back.

True success is more than simply personal accomplishment; it's about leveraging your platform to help others. Mentoring budding entrepreneurs, helping your community, or promoting social issues can increase the effect of your success.

A Call to Action.

Now is the moment to take the initial steps towards creating the company and life you've always wanted. Every successful entrepreneur began where you are today: with a dream and the desire to make it a reality. Use the ideas, skills, and methods in this book as a compass, and believe in your capacity to create something exceptional.

The route to company ownership is about more than simply getting there; it's also about enjoying the ride. So think big, prepare carefully, and act bravely. Your entrepreneurial journey starts now.

Move ahead with confidence, purpose, and unwavering trust in your mission. The world is waiting for something only you can build.

Appendix

This appendix includes extra information, tools, and practical templates to help you along your company ownership path. Use these resources to enhance the methods covered in this book and establish a solid foundation for your enterprise.

1. Business Plan Template.

A business plan is vital for defining your objectives, obtaining investors, and directing your operations. Here's a basic template to help you get started:

Executive Summary:

- Business name and description
- Mission & Vision Statement
- Summary of Products/Services Offered
- Overview of the target market.
- Financial objectives

Market Analysis:
- Industry Overview
- Target client profile
- Competitive analysis
- Market Trends and Opportunities.

Operating Plan:
- Organizational structure (LLC, company, etc.)
- Location and Facilities

Key operating processes:

Marketing Strategy:
- Branding and messaging
- Pricing Strategy
- Sales channels
- Advertising and promotion strategies

Financial Plans:
- Start-up expenses
- Revenue forecasts.
- Expense breakdown

Funding requirements:

2. Goal-setting Framework: SMART Goals

When defining corporate objectives, utilize the SMART framework to ensure they are:

Specific: Clearly state what you aim to accomplish.

Measurable: Include measures for tracking progress.

Set reasonable and achievable objectives.

Relevant: Align your goals with your overall vision and objectives.

Time-bound: Set deadlines to generate a feeling of urgency.

Like this one: "Increase monthly website traffic by 25% within the next three months through targeted social media campaigns and SEO improvements."

3. Financial Resources for Entrepreneurs.

Funding Options:

Small Business Administration (SBA) loans are government-backed loans with competitive conditions.

Crowdfunding platforms include sites like Kickstarter, Indiegogo, and GoFundMe.

Angel Investors and Venture Capital: Seek money from people or businesses interested in your sector.

Business Grants: Look into grants available for startups in your field.

Accounting tools:
- QuickBooks
- Wave Accounting
- Xero

4. Market Research Tools.

Free Resources:
- United States Census Bureau (demographic statistics)
- Google Trends (search trends, consumer interest)

- Social media analytics (Facebook Insights and Instagram Analytics)

Paid Resources:
- Nielsen (consumer behavior insights)
- IBISWorld provides industry reports.
- SEMrush or Ahrefs (tools for SEO and competitor analysis)

5. Legal and Administrative Checklist
- Select a business structure (LLC, single proprietorship, corporation, etc.).
- Register your company name with your state or nation.
- Obtain an EIN (Employer Identification Number) from the IRS, if appropriate.
- Apply for the appropriate licenses and permissions.
- Create a specialized company bank account.

- Secure your company insurance (general liability, property, etc.).

6. Networking and Mentoring Platforms

Local Chambers of Commerce: Join to network with other company owners in your community.

SCORE offers free coaching and support from seasoned entrepreneurs.

LinkedIn Groups: Join conversations and connect with industry colleagues.

Startup Incubators and Accelerators: Discover programs that provide mentoring and investment.

7. Recommended Reading List

Entrepreneurship and Business Management:
- The Lean Startup by Eric Ries
- Good to Great by Jim Collins
- Zero To One by Peter Thiel

Leadership and Teambuilding: Leaders Eat Last by Simon Sinek

Drive: The Surprising Truth About What Motivates Us, by Daniel H. Pink

Personal Development:
- Atomic Habits, by James Clear.
- Stephen R. Covey's "The Seven Habits of Highly Effective People

8. Inspirational Quotes for Entrepreneurs

"The best way to predict the future is to create it." — Peter Drucker

"Success is not final, failure is not fatal: It is the courage to continue that count." — Winston Churchill.

"Entrepreneurship is living a few years of your life like most people won't, so you can spend the rest of your life like most people can't." — Anonymous.

9. Online Marketing Resources.

- Canva: Create professional-looking marketing materials.
- Use Hootsuite or Buffer to schedule and manage social media postings.
- Mailchimp: Set up email marketing campaigns.
- Google Ads and Facebook Ads: Create targeted advertising campaigns.

10. Contact Information and Resources.

Government Resources:
- United States Small Business Administration (SBA): www.sba.gov.
- Internal Revenue Service (IRS) website: www.irs.gov.

Nonprofit and Organisations:
- Score: www.score.org.
- National Association of the Self-Employed (NASE): www.nase.org.

Community forums:
- Reddit Entrepreneurship:

[www.reddit.com/r/Entrepreneur.](www.reddit.com/r/Entrepreneur)

- Quora Business Topics: www.Quora.com

This appendix is intended to serve as a useful resource for you as you embark on your business path. The journey ahead may be difficult, but with preparation, perseverance, and the correct resources, you may attain your goals.

www.ingramcontent.com/pod-product-compliance
Lightning Source LLC
Chambersburg PA
CBHW071059240526
45471CB00016B/2167